NATIONAL
GEOGRAPHIC
KiDS

PUZZLE
BOOK
DOGS

Published by Collins
An imprint of HarperCollins Publishers
Westerhill Road
Bishopbriggs
Glasgow G64 2QT
www.harpercollins.co.uk

HarperCollins Publishers
1st Floor, Watermarque Building, Ringsend Road, Dublin 4, Ireland

In association with National Geographic Partners, LLC

NATIONAL GEOGRAPHIC and the Yellow Border Design are trademarks of the
National Geographic Society, used under license.

First published 2021

ISBN 978-0-00-843049-8

10 9 8 7 6 5 4 3 2 1

Printed in China by RR Donnelley APS Co Ltd.

If you would like to comment on any aspect of this book,
please contact us at the above address or online.
natgeokidsbooks.co.uk
collins.reference@harpercollins.co.uk

Paper from responsible sources.

Acknowledgements

Cover images ©Shutterstock.com

All internal images © Shutterstock.com

NATIONAL GEOGRAPHIC KiDS

PUZZLE BOOK

DOGS

FACT-PACKED FUN

CONTENTS

DOG CARE 42

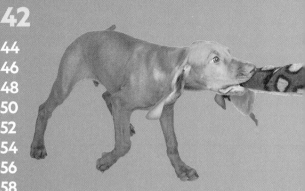

WILD DOGS 60

UNUSUAL DOGS 76

SOLUTIONS 94

BIG DOGS

Let's get started with some fun facts and awesome puzzles about the largest of our canine friends: big dogs!

AFGHAN HOUNDS are also known as 'scented hounds' because they give off a 'musky jasmine' smell, thanks to the scent glands in their cheeks!

Crosswords

Crack the crosswords by solving the clues below. Answers have the same amount of letters as the number in brackets. Can you work out the names of the big dogs using the letters in the shaded squares? See if you are right by flicking to page 94.

Across

1 Woody plant (4)
3 Large American wild cat also known as a cougar (4)
5 Country whose capital is Buenos Aires (9)
6 Very large hairy spider (9)
8 Impressive or incredible (9)
10 Money that is borrowed (4)
11 Border (4)

Down

1 Very attractive (9)
2 African dog-like animal (5)
3 Deep hole in the ground (3)
4 Mass of snow or rock sliding down a mountain (9)
7 One of the senses (5)
9 Nine plus one (3)

AKITAS don't need snow shoes! Because the akita breed originates from the snowy mountains of Japan, they have developed special webbed toes to help them walk on snow!

BOXERS often snore a lot, because of their short snouts! Zzzzzzzzz.

Across

4 E.g. white or pink (6)
6 Another name for a killer whale (4)
7 Viral infection (3)
8 Flightless New Zealand bird (4)
9 Tidy (4)
10 Make free of (3)
11 E.g. sandal (4)
12 _____ Williams: tennis star (6)

Down

1 Fed (9)
2 Large open-air blazes (8)
3 Materials used to wrap goods (9)
5 Game you might play at school (8)

Sudokus

Help the border collie solve the big dog sudokus. Fill in the blank squares so that numbers 1 to 6 appear once in each row, column and 3 x 2 box. See if you are right by flicking to page 94.

A **BORDER COLLIE DOG** has the largest tested memory of any animal – it memorised over 1,000 English words!

					4
4			1		3
		6	4		
		2	5		
3		4			1
2					

DALMATIANS aren't born with spots! They are born white and start to get their trademark black spots when they are a few weeks old.

Wordsearches

Help the German shepherd find other big dogs.
Search left to right, up and down to find the big
dogs listed in the boxes below. See if you
are right by flicking to page 94.

GERMAN SHEPHERDS are sometimes called alsatians.

Afghan hound
boxer
collie
dalmatian
German shepherd
labrador
poodle
sheepdog

e	a	y	q	i	g	t	l	k	m	p	b	i	y
u	d	p	d	m	e	z	r	l	w	u	u	l	u
a	c	u	o	l	r	l	a	b	r	a	d	o	r
p	o	y	g	t	m	a	p	o	o	d	l	e	n
u	l	o	s	f	a	f	f	f	q	f	l	e	r
z	l	s	o	a	n	g	t	d	a	d	t	r	m
w	i	h	j	e	s	h	q	a	u	a	t	s	b
l	e	e	r	w	h	a	a	r	w	l	i	y	h
t	e	e	b	w	e	n	q	u	t	m	d	s	a
c	r	p	o	h	p	h	p	a	n	a	z	u	l
z	c	d	x	r	h	o	o	z	v	t	e	l	k
n	l	o	e	r	e	u	f	i	t	i	r	s	f
o	g	g	r	r	r	n	l	n	r	a	f	r	r
r	b	o	j	b	d	d	z	l	w	n	w	o	f

```
r n e w f o u n d l a n d e
n r t g c e i u m k z n z r
w o d r s e t t e r y t b k
f f r e u k e t h e q i h k
p b i a s w l l n a h z u o
o t h t p h a i s j p u s h
i p c d i x a t w a m y k r
n r h a d y e d u u y f y a
t c o n u o r y m r t s t h
e o w e r o t t w e i l e r
r s c r j k p l h u l s a v
b e h o t w t d z r u e s r
e p o u z r a k i t a s t z
f z w o r r t t q o i i t j
```

akita	Newfoundland
chow chow	pointer
great Dane	rottweiler
husky	setter

GOLDEN RETRIEVERS are known for carrying things very gently in their 'soft mouths'!

13

Mazes

Use your canine instincts to sniff your way around the maze until you reach the exit. See if you are right by flicking to page 95.

OLD ENGLISH SHEEPDOGS are known for their distinctive shaggy coat, and have a very loud and powerful bark! *WOOF!*

Spot the difference

Compare the German shepherd images.
Can you spot the five differences between the photographs?
See if you are right by flicking to page 95.

WELCOME

Guess what?

1. **What breed was Zeus, the world's tallest dog?**
   a. Dalmatian
   b. Boxer
   c. Great Dane

2. **What is the heaviest dog breed?**
   a. English mastiff
   b. Rottweiler
   c. Poodle

3. **When do dalmatians get their spots?**
   a. When they're born
   b. Around 2–3 weeks after birth
   c. Around 1 year old

4. **What is special about Snuppy the Afghan hound?**
   a. First cloned dog
   b. Fastest recorded run
   c. First dog in space

5. **What are alsatians better known as?**
   a. Golden retrievers
   b. German shepherds
   c. Labradors

6. **Which mountain range did Saint Bernards originate from?**
   a. Himalayas
   b. Andes
   c. Alps

7. **What were poodles orignally bred for?**
   a. Guarding
   b. Hunting
   c. Fashio

8. **What is special about akitas' toes?**
   a. They are webbed
   b. They have three on each paw
   c. They are different colours

9. **The famous dog 'Lassie' was which breed?**
   a. Setter
   b. Collie
   c. Pointer

10. **How tall do Irish wolfhounds grow?**
    a. Around 40 cm
    b. Around 80 cm
    c. Around 120 cm

POINTERS got their name because they can be trained to freeze and point to something with their nose, which used to help hunters.

Can you guess the answers to the questions below?
Check your answers by flicking to page 95.

POODLES get their name from the German word meaning 'to splash'. Originally, sections of poodles' fur were shaved off to reduce the weight of wet fur in the water, but fur was left around the organs, head and joints to keep them warm.

Close-ups

Big dog breeds come in all kinds of different styles. Can you match the fluffy canine close-ups on the left with the pictures below? See if you are right by flicking to page 95.

1 Bearded collie

2 Bernese mountain dog

3 Saint Bernard

4 Irish setter

5 Kuvasz

6 Rough collie

Word jumbles

T A M A L D A N I

E T I V R E R E R

O R D A R A L B

SIBERIAN HUSKIES are often born with a condition called heterochromia, where their eyes are different colours!

Rearrange the jumbled letters to form five popular big dog breeds.
See if you are right by flicking to page 95.

ROTTWEILERS were bred with a strong build to pull carts and herd cattle. When trains came along and took their jobs, these working dogs nearly became extinct!

D O L P E O

M E G A R N

D E H P E R S H

SMALL DOGS

Get ready for fascinating facts and puzzles on some of the world's coolest small dogs.

FRENCH BULLDOGS can't swim because of their short bodies and large heads.

Crosswords

Crack the crosswords by solving the clues below. Answers have the same amount of letters as the number in brackets. Can you work out the names of the small dog breeds using the letters in the shaded squares? See if you are right by flicking to page 96.

BRITISH BULLDOGS have a short snout which makes them prone to breathing problems. This can result in snorting and passing wind!

Across

1 Company that delivers post (5,4)
5 Nothing (3)
7 Game of chance (7)
8 Respects (7)
11 Brown colour (3)
12 Capital city of Scotland (9)

Down

1 .... energy: energy that comes from natural resources (9)
2 Shout or scream loudly (4)
3 Bale (anag.) (4)
4 Maze (9)
6 Gaze at steadily (5)
9 Small; tiny (4)

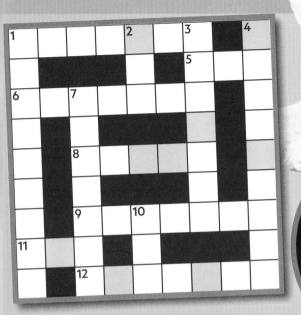

BICHON FRISE
were reportedly one of the French King, Henry III's, favourite dog breeds. He even wore a special basket around his neck so he could take his fluffy lap dogs everywhere with him!

Across

1 Take part in a religious ceremony (7)
5 Be in debt to (3)
6 Type of computer (7)
8 Of the same value (5)
9 Merit (7)
11 Great serve in tennis (3)
12 Mammals with long ears (7)

Down

1 Day before Thursday (9)
2 Very warm (3)
3 Liked by many people (7)
4 Eight hens (anag.) (9)
7 Slim (7)
10 Cry (3)

Sudokus

Help the King Charles spaniel solve the sudokus.
Fill in the blank squares so that numbers 1 to 6
appear once in each row, column and 3 x 2 box.
See if you are right by flicking to page 96.

2	3				
		5			
	5	3			6
	2		5	1	
			6		
				5	2

KING CHARLES SPANIELS were
loved so much by King
Charles II that legend says
he made it illegal to ban the
dog from any building,
even the houses of
parliament!

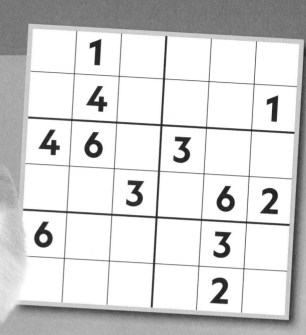

According to some Welsh legends, **CORGIS** are 'enchanted dogs'. It is said magical creatures like fairies and elves use corgis to pull their carriages during the night.

Wordsearches

BEAGLES are very loud dogs known for barking and howling. Even their name is thought to come from the French 'bee guele', which means 'loudmouth'!

```
b x y c b e x t r i p i a o
i z e o t y t f p f d c o g
c b a r i c f u e q a i t p
h p u g e c c v a a c j s z
o z o i a h d n i k h a d b
n z h l g r r l l r s c i u
f u e e n t s a l o h k v l
r k r m j r f p o u u r a l
i s p a n i e l i p n u k d
s x o b u t s y c w d s s o
e r e t t r s n q n l s a g
b o s t o n t e r r i e r r
i s i i e b z t h a p l q e
w u o s e f t a x p f l t h
```

bichon frise
Boston terrier
bulldog
corgi
dachshund
Jack russell
pug
spaniel

Help the beagle sniff out other small dog breeds. Search left to right, up and down to find the small dog breeds listed in the boxes below. See if you are right by flicking to page 96.

o	t	r	t	z	p	o	j	v	d	t	y	s	t
e	h	c	s	a	o	p	s	s	t	t	y	x	n
r	s	h	o	s	m	k	y	z	o	s	b	p	s
w	a	i	q	t	e	i	n	l	p	w	e	h	h
i	o	h	i	l	r	g	h	s	b	s	a	b	i
s	m	u	k	y	a	a	r	s	a	r	g	h	h
p	f	a	d	g	n	z	h	k	x	a	l	v	t
u	u	h	c	q	i	x	w	i	p	a	e	c	z
g	y	u	s	t	a	d	j	q	u	d	m	s	u
y	f	a	o	i	n	y	k	x	o	p	t	s	o
n	u	p	k	s	b	g	g	t	p	o	b	o	j
c	e	s	k	y	t	e	r	r	i	e	r	k	c
p	u	t	t	o	c	s	o	e	h	p	l	f	b
o	f	k	p	e	k	i	n	g	e	s	e	k	v

beagle
cesky terrier
chihuahua
pekingese
pomeranian
shih tzu

A **DACHSHUND** named Waldi was the first official mascot of the summer Olympic Games, in 1972.

31

Mazes

Zoom like a greyhound around the maze until you reach the exit.
See if you are right by flicking to page 97.

MINIATURE SCHNAUZERS have long moustaches to protect their face when they hunt rats!

z

ITALIAN GREYHOUNDS are the smallest of the breeds known as sighthounds. They are good at catching prey because of their speed and excellent peripheral vision.

Spot the difference

Compare the two small dog images.
Can you spot the five differences between the photographs?
See if you are right by flicking to page 97.

Guess what?

1. What breed is Milly, the world's smallest dog?
   a. Yorkshire terrier
   b. Chihuahua
   c. Pomeranian

2. What dog's name means 'little lion'?
   a. Shih tzu
   b. Pekingese
   c. Dachshund

3. Queen Elizabeth II is known to keep which breed of dog?
   a. Bichon frise
   b. British bulldog
   c. Corgi

4. Beagles belong to what group of dogs?
   a. Hound
   b. Terrier
   c. Gun

5. A Scottish terrier can be found in which family board game?
   a. Mouse Trap
   b. Monopoly
   c. Battleship

6. Jack Russell terriers can jump how high?
   a. 1.0 m
   b. 1.5 m
   c. 2.0 m

7. Which of these dog breeds cannot swim?
   a. French bulldog
   b. Poodle
   c. Cocker spaniel

8. Which country did beagles originate from?
   a. France
   b. Germany
   c. United Kingdom

9. The most common colour for miniature schnauzers is?
   a. Golden
   b. Salt and pepper
   c. Brown

10. The average pug weighs between?
    a. 3-6 kg
    b. 6-9 kg
    c. 9-12 kg

PUGS are a very old breed and were kept by Buddhist monks in Tibetan temples!

Can you guess the answers to the small dog questions below? Check your answers by flicking to page 97.

SCOTTISH TERRIERS are well known for being featured in the board game Monopoly.

Close-ups

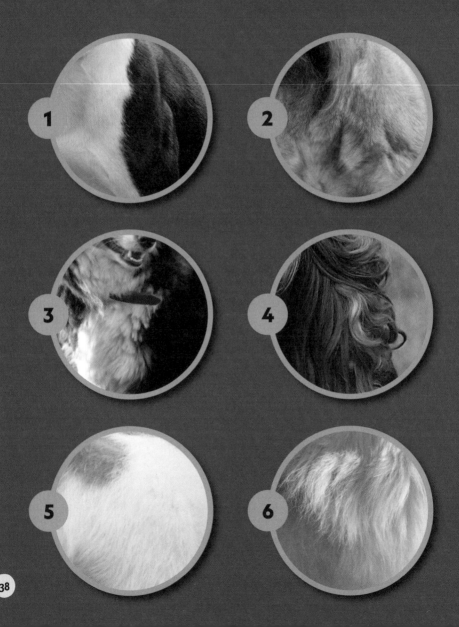

Small dog breeds come in all kinds of different styles. Can you match the cute canine close-ups on the left with the pictures below? See if you are right by flicking to page 97.

1 Cavalier King Charles spaniel

2 Cesky terrier

3 Boston terrier

4 Miniature Jack Russell

5 Pekingese

6 Shetland sheepdog

Word jumbles

Rearrange the jumbled letters to form five popular small dog breeds. See if you are right by flicking to page 97.

G K N I

C A L S E R H

N P A S L E I

C I O H N B
F S R E I

WEST HIGHLAND WHITE TERRIERS are a very talkative breed, first bred to bark loudly so their owners could hear them even when underground!

SHIH TZU translates to 'little lion', these dogs get their name from a Tibetan legend of a small dog who turned into a lion.

I U T M R A N I E

C Z H N S E R U A

C F E R N H

O B L U G D L

I A T L N A I

U N H D O E R G Y

DOG CARE

Learn about how to look after your forver friends with these dog care facts and puzzles!

DID YOU KNOW that dogs can learn from human emotions? A dog may be more likely to play with a toy if they've already seen their owner play with that toy and display positive emotions!

Crosswords

Crack the crosswords by solving the clues below. Answers have the same amount of letters as the number in brackets. Can you work out the dog care keywords by using the letters in the shaded squares? See if you are right by flicking to page 98.

The amount a dog needs to eat changes as it grows up. Puppies need four or more small meals each day, but older dogs can usually be fed two or three larger meals a day.

Across

1 Cause friction (3)
5 Very great (7)
7 A large expanse of water (3)
8 Tell a story (7)
9 Person who lives in a country (7)
11 Pigment that changes the colour of something (3)
12 Solar _____ : this temporarily hides the sun from view (7)
13 Sprint (3)

Down

1 Admired or highly regarded (9)
2 Jack and the _____ : fairy tale (9)
3 Amount left over (9)
4 Nine plus eight (9)
6 Rat (anag.) (3)
10 Coat fastener (3)

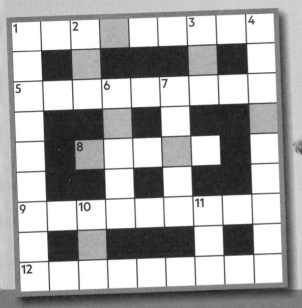

Some human foods are poisonous to dogs. Keep dogs away from chocolate, onions, garlic, grapes and raisins.

Across

1 Flying vehicle (9)
5 Neil _____ : first person to walk on the moon (9)
8 Bacteria (5)
9 Opposite of forwards (9)
12 Approximated the result (9)

Down

1 Free; not occupied (9)
2 Edge of a cup (3)
3 In the past (3)
4 Absorbed or immersed in (9)
6 Snake (anag.) (5)
7 Type of dance (5)
10 A bed for a baby (3)
11 Rodent with a long tail (3)

Sudokus

Solve the dog care sudokus. Fill in the blank squares so that numbers 1 to 6 appear once in each row, column and 3 x 2 box. See if you are right by flicking to page 98.

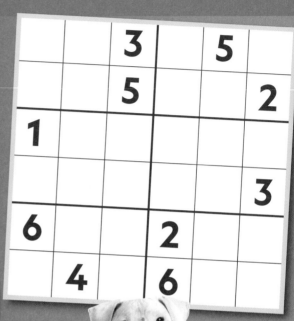

		3		5	
		5			2
1					
					3
6			2		
	4		6		

Dog's coats contain special oils to keep their fur strong and shiny. That's why most healthy dogs shouldn't take baths more than once per fortnight, because over-bathing can wash the natural oils away!

Just like humans, dogs need to have their nails trimmed every so often to stop them growing too long.

Grid 1 (6×6)

		3		5	6
	2			4	1
5	1			6	
6	5		1		

Grid 2 (6×6)

	4		5		
				6	
		5			6
2			3		
	1				
		3		2	

Wordsearches

Help the pooches crack the wordsearches to find dog care words.
Search left to right, up and down to find the words listed in the
boxes below. See if you are right by flicking to page 98.

brush
exercise
fetch
grooming
healthy
play
veterinarian
washing

a	i	a	y	f	y	a	o	w	b	r	u	s	h
c	k	i	f	e	l	l	a	t	p	r	s	o	b
v	s	r	z	t	b	g	z	q	u	b	a	q	e
e	a	o	u	c	e	r	x	m	s	j	k	p	n
t	w	t	y	h	g	o	e	p	c	t	t	t	i
e	a	p	u	r	r	o	o	x	l	k	e	k	u
r	s	b	r	u	f	m	u	i	m	i	x	d	p
i	h	a	t	c	v	i	o	a	s	t	e	s	s
n	i	e	h	t	s	n	y	j	t	u	r	i	i
a	n	s	l	a	s	g	p	l	a	y	c	l	z
r	g	d	b	h	o	i	a	i	v	w	i	r	s
i	m	w	n	a	c	u	t	p	s	r	s	b	u
a	l	k	u	a	n	c	a	t	y	j	e	a	t
n	t	o	a	a	q	s	h	e	a	l	t	h	y

It's well known that
dogs are colour blind, but
they don't see in black and
white. They can see colours,
just not as many as humans!
They can see blue and
yellow, but not red and
green.

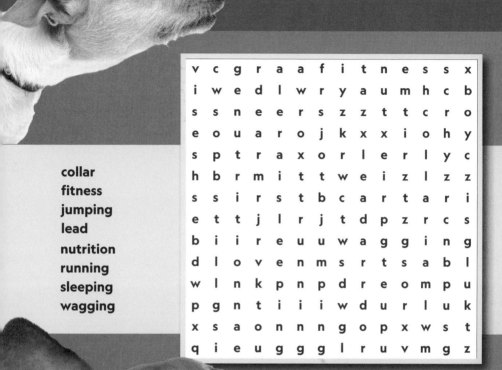

collar
fitness
jumping
lead
nutrition
running
sleeping
wagging

v	c	g	r	a	a	f	i	t	n	e	s	s	x
i	w	e	d	l	w	r	y	a	u	m	h	c	b
s	s	n	e	e	r	s	z	z	t	t	c	r	o
e	o	u	a	r	o	j	k	x	x	i	o	h	y
s	p	t	r	a	x	o	r	l	e	r	l	y	c
h	b	r	m	i	t	t	w	e	i	z	l	z	z
s	s	i	r	s	t	b	c	a	r	t	a	r	i
e	t	t	j	l	r	j	t	d	p	z	r	c	s
b	i	i	r	e	u	u	w	a	g	g	i	n	g
d	l	o	v	e	n	m	s	r	t	s	a	b	l
w	l	n	k	p	n	p	d	r	e	o	m	p	u
p	g	n	t	i	i	i	w	d	u	r	l	u	k
x	s	a	o	n	n	n	g	o	p	x	w	s	t
q	i	e	u	g	g	g	l	r	u	v	m	g	z

Dogs have some super senses! A dog's sense of smell can be more than 10,000 times better than a human's. Also, they can see ultraviolet light, sense Earth's natural magnetic fields, and can hear ultrasound waves!

Mazes

Whizz around the maze until you reach the exit. See if you are right by flicking to page 99.

Dogs wag their tails for all kinds of reasons. There's a whole tail wagging language that many people interpret differently. Some studies say a dog wagging its tail to the right means they're happy, but to the left means they might be frightened!

Most dogs need at least 30 minutes of exercise per day, but some active breeds need a lot more, and can exercise for over 2 hours daily!

Spot the difference

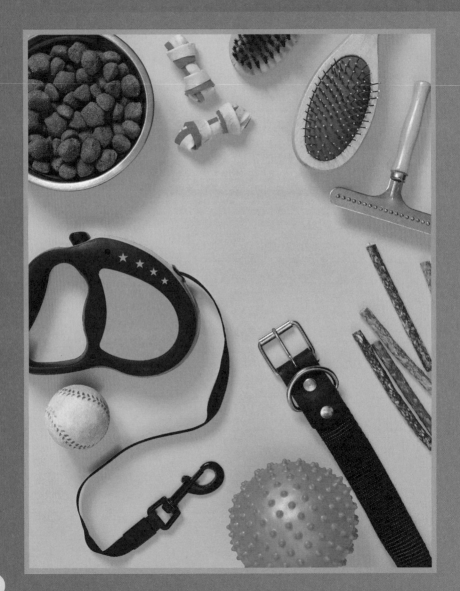

Compare the two images.
Can you spot the five differences between the photographs?
See if you are right by flicking to page 99.

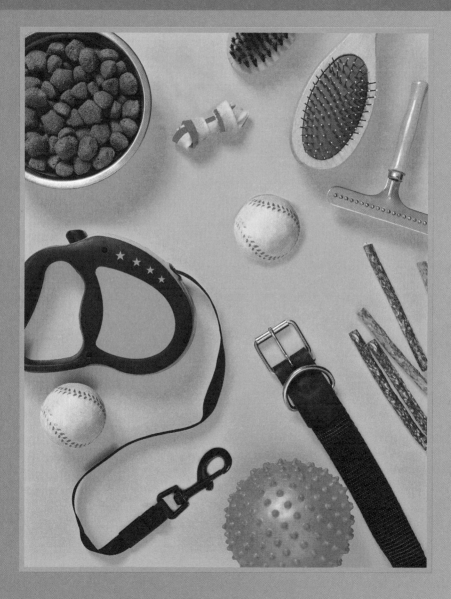

Guess what?

1. **What is the largest dog show in the world called?**
   a. World Dog Show
   b. Crufts
   c. Westminster Kennel Club Dog Show

2. **Which dog breed is most intelligent?**
   a. Border collie
   b. Italian greyhound
   c. German shepherd

3. **The largest dog walk recorded involved how many dogs?**
   a. 224
   b. 2,847
   c. 22,742

4. **How heavy was the world's largest dog biscuit?**
   a. 27.43 kg
   b. 279.87 kg
   c. 872.69 kg

5. **Finley, a golden retriever, holds the dog world record for?**
   a. Balancing treats on his nose
   b. Fastest 30 m bicycle ride
   c. Most tennis balls held in mouth

6. **A dog's sense of smell can be how much better than a human's?**
   a. 10 times
   b. 100 times
   c. 10,000 times

7. **Which of these foods should you not feed dogs?**
   a. Chocolate
   b. Carrots
   c. Chicken

8. **The average dog can learn how many words?**
   a. 75
   b. 165
   c. 425

9. **Which of these dog breeds are most popular in the United Kingdom?**
   a. Labrador retriever
   b. Chow chow
   c. Pug

10. **What colours can dogs not see?**
    a. Yellow and blue
    b. Red and green
    c. Blue and red

A dog lying belly-up with their tongue out is very happy dog! Belly an tongue displays togeth are a good sign that a do enjoying your company.

Can you guess the answers to the dog care questions below?
Check your answers by flicking to page 99.

A sign of a relaxed and happy dog is if their eyes and eyelids are very relaxed around you and they blink a lot.

Close-ups

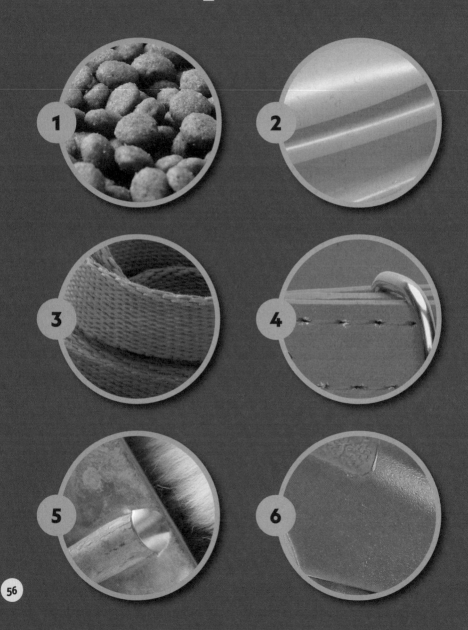

Can you match the dog care close-ups on the left with the pictures below? See if you are right by flicking to page 99.

1 lead

2 collar

3 brush

4 toys

5 clippers

6 food

Word jumbles

T E B S   N I   O S W H

G A G I W T S E
L A T I

S B T E
O R G E D O M

Millions of dog lovers from around the world attend dog shows each year. Many people pay thousands of pounds to compete even though the competitions' cash prizes tend to be small. They usually do it just for the pride of winning award titles!

Rearrange the jumbled letters to form five common dog show categories. See if you are right by flicking to page 99.

S T E B

R I T K C

T U E S T C

U P Y P P

Dogs at dog shows can be judged on various criteria, including body or muscle size and proportion, eye shape and colour, head shape, tail arch, and coat texture, colour and length!

WILD DOGS

Get your canines into these fun facts and puzzles all about the craziest of canines: wild dogs!

The world is full of wondeful wild canines, from howling wolves to furry Arctic foxes.

Crosswords

Crack the crosswords by solving the clues below. Answers have the same amount of letters as the number in brackets. Can you work out the names of the wild dogs using the letters in the shaded squares? See if you are right by flicking to page 100.

AFRICAN WILD DOGS have incredible endurance. They can run for three hours or more while chasing prey!

Across

4 Summer month (6)
6 Ready to eat (of fruit) (4)
7 Present (4)
8 Large black bird (4)
9 Very cold (3)
10 Wife of an uncle (4)
11 Colour of a lemon (6)

Down

1 Items such as sofas and tables (9)
2 Amount (8)
3 Loud bang (9)
5 Vehicle similar to a bike but with three wheels (8)

(6,3)

BAT-EARED FOXES love to eat termites. The insects make up 80% of their diet.

Across

1 Gesture or sound that conveys information (6)
6 Building (9)
7 Garden of ____ : Biblical location (4)
8 Put paper around something (4)
9 Type of statue (9)
11 Person currently in first place (6)

Down

1 Feeling of uncertainty; tension (8)
2 Very attractive (8)
3 A part of a curve (3)
4 Encircle (8)
5 A period of 366 days (4,4)
10 A baked dish with a top and base made from pastry (3)

Sudokus

Help the jackal solve the sudokus. Fill in the blank squares so that numbers 1 to 6 appear once in each row, column and 3 x 2 box. See if you are right by flicking to page 100.

	3	5			4
2					
				1	2
4	1				
					5
6			3	2	

BLACK-BACKED JACKALS are pack dogs whose pups stay with their family to help raise new generations.

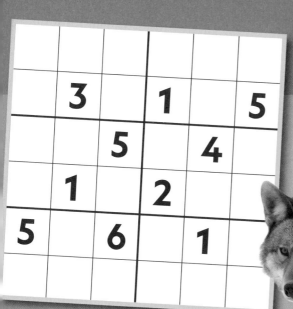

Puzzle 1

	3		1		5
		5		4	
	1		2		
5		6		1	

Puzzle 2

1	2				
				1	
6			4		5
5		4			1
	5				
				2	6

MALE COYOTES have been known to travel 160 km to find a territory with enough food.

Wordsearches

Sniff out the wild dog terms in the wordsearches below. Search left to right, up and down to find the wild words in the boxes below. See if you are right by flicking to page 100.

Arctic fox
corsac fox
coyote
grey wolf
howl
jackal
pack
wildlife

o	i	i	r	s	h	w	u	p	i	i	r	u	q
u	r	o	l	d	r	i	r	s	t	l	u	k	t
l	a	m	a	e	q	w	i	l	d	l	i	f	e
v	d	s	x	s	i	o	r	y	f	e	f	y	o
m	r	t	r	a	c	o	r	s	a	c	f	o	x
j	a	x	q	r	t	k	j	r	e	t	d	u	p
a	p	s	b	c	u	o	s	e	p	g	q	n	g
c	a	t	j	t	n	p	s	c	o	y	o	t	e
k	c	g	r	i	g	h	g	h	s	b	v	l	y
a	k	r	i	c	f	o	h	t	e	q	z	j	c
l	n	j	t	f	z	w	s	a	b	m	r	y	a
r	s	x	u	o	b	l	r	o	u	b	a	k	p
k	s	i	b	x	i	g	r	e	y	w	o	l	f
v	s	q	x	e	n	u	t	q	v	l	v	r	a

CORSAC FOXES

live in burrows but aren't that good at digging, so they have been known to steal other animals' burrows for themselves.

GREY WOLVES are the largest living wild dog. Some say that wolves howl at the moon but they actually howl to communicate with other wolves, both within their own pack and to warn off other wolf packs.

h	o	e	y	t	u	f	e	r	a	l	p	i	e
u	t	v	d	x	y	o	c	k	h	l	h	l	o
n	p	p	t	v	i	e	o	o	s	k	s	c	i
t	o	h	r	a	r	e	g	u	d	r	t	d	r
e	h	q	l	w	a	o	s	s	t	i	f	a	
r	b	a	t	e	a	r	e	d	f	o	x	e	c
s	f	c	k	c	l	s	o	t	k	y	u	n	c
q	x	a	s	o	g	o	c	t	w	s	w	n	o
m	a	n	e	d	w	o	l	f	a	s	w	e	o
k	o	i	h	s	t	w	h	n	p	r	o	c	n
i	s	n	w	r	m	r	f	w	s	w	o	f	d
r	e	e	i	i	r	q	t	c	l	t	h	o	o
f	t	t	l	b	t	g	c	o	b	n	c	x	g
z	r	x	d	q	u	j	t	f	a	l	f	r	u

bat-eared fox
canine
fennec fox
feral
hunters
maned wolf
raccoon dog
wild

Mazes

Prowl like a fox around the maze until you reach the exit. See if you are right by flicking to page 101.

MANED WOLVES are the tallest members of the wild canine family. Their long legs help them see over long grasses while hunting in their native South American habitats.

FENNEC FOXES are the smallest members of the dog family, weighing as little as 1 kg. That's about the same weight as a guinea pig!

Spot the difference

Compare the two wild dog images.
Can you spot the five differences between the photographs?
See if you are right by flicking to page 101.

Guess what?

1. **Arctic foxes can survive in temperatures as low as?**
   a. -25°C
   b. -50°C
   c. -75°C

2. **Which wild dog is know for its exceptional endurance?**
   a. Bat-eared fox
   b. Raccoon dog
   c. African wild dog

3. **What are coyotes very good at?**
   a. Playing catch
   b. Swimming
   c. Running backwards

4. **How long can wolves go between meals?**
   a. 12 hours
   b. 12 days
   c. 12 weeks

5. **What is the smallest member of the canine family?**
   a. Fennec fox
   b. Raccoon dog
   c. Coyote

6. **80% of which wild dog's diet is made up of termites?**
   a. Black-backed jackal
   b. Grey wolf
   c. Bat-eared fox

7. **The corsac fox is native to?**
   a. Central Asia
   b. North America
   c. Eastern Europe

8. **What is a group of wild dogs called?**
   a. A herd
   b. A pack
   c. A pride

9. **How tall can the maned wolf grow?**
   a. 30 cm
   b. 60 cm
   c. 90 cm

10. **Where in the world would you find the simien jackal?**
    a. Ethiopia
    b. South Korea
    c. Chile

RACCOON DOGS are native to east Asia.

Can you guess the answers to the wild dog questions below?
Check your answers by flicking to page 101.

SIMIEN JACKALS or 'Ethiopian wolves' are one of the world's rarest wild canine species!

Word jumbles

Rearrange the jumbled letters to form the names of five wild canines. See if you are right by flicking to page 101.

C R C A I T

O X F

N S I I M E

J C A K L A

WOLVES
can survive without eating for more than a week.

R Y E G
O W L F

N N E E C F
F X O

T O O C Y E

UNUSUAL DOGS

Let's not forget these curious dogs! Are you ready for some more puzzles and canine facts on unusual dog breeds?

CHINESE CRESTED DOGS are a hairless dog breed, however, there are two varieties – one with fur and one with very little fur! Both types can be born in the same litter.

Crosswords

Crack the crosswords by solving the clues below. Answers have the same amount of letters as the number in brackets. Can you work out the names of the unusual dogs using the letters in the shaded squares? See if you are right by flicking to page 102.

Across

4 Australian marsupials (9)
6 ___ Vegas: famous city in America (3)
8 Topic (anag.) (5)
9 More knowledgeable (5)
10 National Health Service (abbrev) (3)
12 Occasionally or once in a while (9)

Down

1 Facts and statistics (4)
2 Best-loved (9)
3 Gone off (of food) (6)
5 Put these on before your shoes (5)
6 _____ Hamilton: racing driver (5)
7 _____ Street: children's TV show (6)
11 Back part of the foot (4)

BEDLINGTON TERRIERS are fluffy dogs who love to dig and exercise regularly.

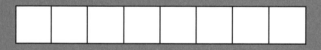

DANDIE DINMONT TERRIERS are known for the dashing curls on the top of their head. They're a very rare breed of terrier with only 300 pups born per year worldwide!

Across

4 What your hand is part of (3)
6 A repeated decorative design (7)
7 Room for young children (7)
8 A type of porridge (7)
10 Prepared for exams (7)
11 A large vehicle that carries passengers by road (3)

Down

1 _____ SquarePants: cartoon character (9)
2 Move a spoon around in a liquid to mix it (4)
3 Investigator (9)
4 ____ Murray: British tennis star (4)
5 A preserve made from citrus fruit that is similar to jam (9)
8 These are used to row a boat (4)
9 Opposite of difficult (4)

Sudokus

Help the bergamasco solve the sudokus. Fill in the blank squares so that numbers 1 to 6 appear once in each row, column and 3 x 2 box. See if you are right by flicking to page 102.

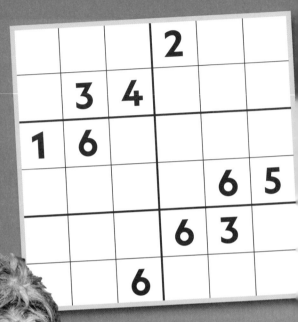

BERGAMASCOS have matted hair that resembles a canine mop!

KOMONDOR is the name for one of these woolly dogs. Komondorok is the name for two or more!

Wordsearches

Sniff out unusual dog terms in the wordsearches below. Search left to right, up and down to find the words listed in the boxes below. See if you are right by flicking to page 102.

See if you are right by flicking to page 102.

AMERICAN HAIRLESS TERRIERS were the first hairless breed to be developed in the USA.

affenpinscher
Chinese crested
hairless
peculiar
puli
unusual
woolly
xoloitzcuintli

j	a	q	x	p	e	c	u	l	i	a	r	z	h
t	f	u	o	e	u	n	u	s	u	a	l	n	i
t	f	t	l	d	j	t	s	r	r	h	t	x	g
l	e	e	o	s	w	z	p	d	r	a	r	c	s
o	n	a	i	u	m	w	p	q	o	i	a	f	r
p	p	r	t	v	s	j	o	z	u	r	s	j	c
u	i	j	z	a	e	f	u	d	v	l	v	e	h
l	n	r	c	g	n	e	d	r	y	e	m	b	r
i	s	g	u	w	b	d	a	o	a	s	q	i	s
e	c	x	i	t	q	e	m	e	h	s	b	m	s
c	h	i	n	e	s	e	c	r	e	s	t	e	d
j	e	n	t	t	l	l	h	u	g	m	a	t	t
u	r	s	l	e	e	b	s	g	q	f	n	j	d
m	n	t	i	w	o	o	l	l	y	l	o	o	r

i	l	o	w	c	h	e	n	b	b	r	s	o	i
a	c	t	b	e	r	g	a	m	a	s	c	o	p
n	u	e	o	r	p	t	c	o	e	i	t	f	n
u	d	b	h	t	p	u	b	r	b	p	k	p	y
r	m	t	r	u	l	x	u	j	a	e	a	r	u
e	h	t	l	a	s	i	l	s	t	o	k	a	t
k	v	y	u	s	t	i	l	d	s	u	c	o	k
t	a	c	e	v	r	v	t	e	u	p	m	o	o
h	m	u	s	x	i	a	e	b	o	c	d	e	m
a	d	r	b	e	k	y	r	j	i	l	a	v	o
i	p	l	z	v	i	a	r	b	r	s	m	m	n
r	a	y	n	p	n	r	i	l	p	c	p	e	d
y	b	t	q	o	g	b	e	t	e	p	i	r	o
s	t	r	a	n	g	e	r	c	s	u	w	p	r

bergamasco

bull terrier

curly

hairy

komondor

lowchen

strange

striking

XOLOITZCUINTLI
(show-low-itz-queent-ly)
statues can be found
in Mexican tombs
that are over 3000
years old!

Mazes

Paw your way around the maze until you reach the exit. See if you are right by flicking to page 103.

CHOW CHOWS are from northern China. Another name for a chow chow is 'songshi quan' which means 'puffy lion dog'.

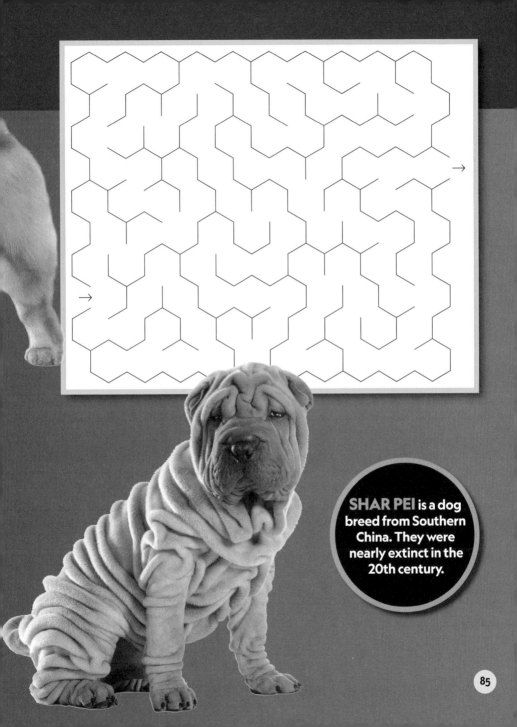

SHAR PEI is a dog breed from Southern China. They were nearly extinct in the 20th century.

Compare the two unusual dog images.
Can you spot the five differences between the photographs?
See if you are right by flicking to page 103.

Guess what?

1. **Which dog has a blue tongue?**
   a. Chow chow
   b. Boston terrier
   c. Basset hound

2. **How many types of hair do bergamascos have?**
   a. One
   b. Two
   c. Three

3. **American hairless terriers were first bred in what year?**
   a. 1827
   b. 1972
   c. 2012

4. **The name shar pei translates to?**
   a. Sand skin
   b. Pebble skin
   c. Grassy skin

5. **Tigger, a bloodhound, has the worlds longest what?**
   a. Tail
   b. Ears
   c. Snout

6. **Where do komondorok originate?**
   a. Canada
   b. Spain
   c. Hungary

7. **Which dog looks similar to a lamb?**
   a. Bedlington terrier
   b. Chinese crested dog
   c. Maltese

8. **Fang, in the *Harry Potter* movies, is played by which breed of dog?**
   a. Newfoundland
   b. Neapolitan mastiff
   c. Great Dane

9. **Affenpinschers have what type of coat?**
   a. Smooth
   b. Wire
   c. Curly

10. **Basenji dogs do not bark, they?**
    a. Purr
    b. Neigh
    c. Yodel

NEAPOLITAN MASTIFF is an Italian dog breed. They have distinctively wrinkly and droopy faces.

Can you guess the answers to the unusual dog questions below?
Check your answers by flicking to page 103.

BULL TERRIERS have egg-shaped faces and triangular eyes.

Close-ups

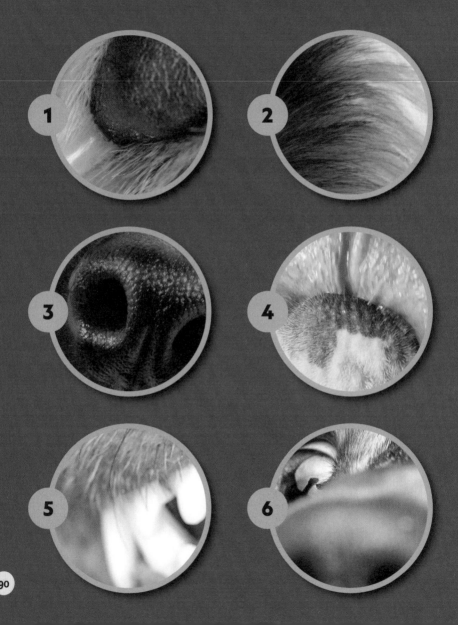

Can you match the dog body part close-ups on the left with the pictures below? See if you are right by flicking to page 103.

1 Nose

2 Tongue

3 Paw

4 Teeth

5 Eye

6 Tail

Word jumbles

Rearrange the jumbled letters to form the names of five
unusual dog breeds. See if you are right by flicking to page 103.

S R H A

I E P

H E I C N E S

R C D T E E S

AFFENPINSCHERS
are sometimes referred
to as monkey terriers.

BLOODHOUNDS have large floppy ears. The longest bloodhound ears ever recorded were 34.9 cm!

R O O M N O D K

W O C H   O W C H

B O D U O O N D H L

SOLUTIONS

Pages 8-9

B	U	S	H		P	U	M	A
E		Y		I			V
A	R	G	E	N	T	I	N	A
U		N					L
T	A	R	A	N	T	U	L	A
I				A			N
F	A	N	T	A	S	T	I	C
U			E		T		H
L	O	A	N		E	D	G	E

Keyword: LABRADOR

	N		B				P	
C	O	L	O	U	R		A	
	U		N		O	R	C	A
	R		F	L	U		K	
K	I	W	I		N	E	A	T
	S		R	I	D		G	
S	H	O	E		E		I	
	E		S	E	R	E	N	A
	D				S		G	

Keyword: AKITA

Pages 10-11

6	1	3	2	5	4
4	2	5	1	6	3
5	3	6	4	1	2
1	4	2	5	3	6
3	5	4	6	2	1
2	6	1	3	4	5

3	4	1	2	6	5
6	2	5	3	1	4
1	6	4	5	2	3
2	5	3	6	4	1
4	3	6	1	5	2
5	1	2	4	3	6

5	3	1	4	6	2
4	2	6	3	1	5
2	1	4	6	5	3
3	6	5	1	2	4
1	5	3	2	4	6
6	4	2	5	3	1

Pages 12-13

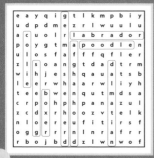

Pages 14-15

Pages 16-17

Page 18

1. c. Great Dane
2. a. English mastiff
3. b. Around 2–3 weeks after birth
4. a. First cloned dog
5. b. German shepherds
6. c. Alps
7. b. Hunting
8. a. They are webbed
9. b. Collie
10. b. Around 80 cm

Pages 20-21

1 – 6 Rough collie
2 – 1 Bearded collie
3 – 2 Bernese mountain dog
4 – 5 Kuvasz
5 – 4 Irish setter
6 – 3 Saint Bernard

Pages 22-23

Dalmatian
Retreiver
Labrador
Poodle
German shepherd

SOLUTIONS

Pages 26-27

Keyword: BEAGLE

Keyword: CHIHUAHUA

Pages 28-29

2	3	6	1	4	5
4	1	5	3	2	6
1	5	3	2	6	4
6	2	4	5	1	3
5	4	2	6	3	1
3	6	1	4	5	2

2	1	5	6	4	3
3	4	6	2	5	1
4	6	2	3	1	5
1	5	3	4	6	2
6	2	1	5	3	4
5	3	4	1	2	6

1	5	6	3	4	2
4	3	2	5	6	1
5	2	3	4	1	6
6	4	1	2	5	3
2	6	5	1	3	4
3	1	4	6	2	5

Pages 30-31

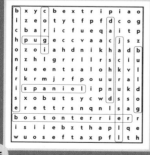

Pages 32-33

Pages 34-35

Page 36

1. b. Chihuahua
2. a. Shih tzu
3. c. Corgi
4. a. Hound
5. b. Monopoly

6. b. 1.5 m
7. a. French bulldog
8. c. United Kingdom
9. b. Salt and pepper
10. b. 6-9 kg

Pages 38-39

1-3 Boston terrier
2-2 Cesky terrier
3-6 Shetland
     sheepdog

4-1 Cavalier King
     Charles spaniel
5-4 Miniature Jack
     Russell
6-5 Pekingese

Pages 40-41

King Charles spaniel
Bichon frise
Miniature schnauzer
French bulldog
Italian greyhound

SOLUTIONS

Pages 44-45

R	U	B			R		S
E		E	X	T	R	E	M	E
S	E	A		A		M		V
P		N	A	R	R	A	T	E
E		S			I		N		T
C	I	T	I	Z	E	N		T
T		A		I		D	Y	E
E	C	L	I	P	S	E		E
D		K			R	U	N

Keyword: EXERCISE

A	E	R	O	P	L	A	N	E
V		I			G			N
A	R	M	S	T	R	O	N	G
I			N		U			R
L		G	E	R	M	S		O
A			A		B			S
B	A	C	K	W	A	R	D	S
L		O			A			E
E	S	T	I	M	A	T	E	D

Keyword: GROOMING

Pages 46-47

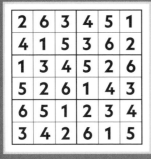

2	6	3	4	5	1
4	1	5	3	6	2
1	3	4	5	2	6
5	2	6	1	4	3
6	5	1	2	3	4
3	4	2	6	1	5

2	6	5	4	1	3
1	4	3	2	5	6
3	2	6	5	4	1
5	1	4	3	6	2
6	5	2	1	3	4
4	3	1	6	2	5

3	4	6	5	1	2
5	2	1	4	6	3
1	3	5	2	4	6
2	6	4	3	5	1
4	1	2	6	3	5
6	5	3	1	2	4

Pages 48-49

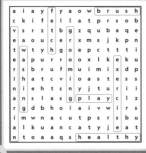

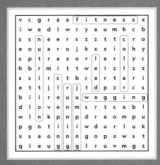

Pages 50–51

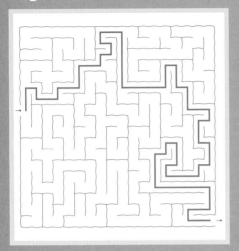

Pages 52–53

Page 54

1. b. Crufts
2. a. Border collie
3. c. 22,742
4. b. 279.87 kg
5. c. Most tennis balls held in mouth
6. c. 10,000 times
7. a. Chocolate
8. b. 165
9. a. Labrador retriever
10. b. Red and green

Pages 56–57

1 – 6 food
2 – 4 toys
3 – 1 lead
4 – 2 collar
5 – 3 brush
6 – 5 clippers

Pages 58–59

Best in show
Waggiest tail
Best groomed
Best trick
Cutest puppy

SOLUTIONS

Pages 62–63

Keyword: ARCTIC FOX

Keyword: COYOTE

Pages 64–65

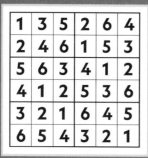

Pages 66–67

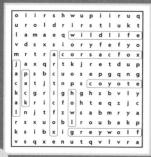

Pages 68-69

Pages 70-71

Page 72

1. b. -50°C
2. c. African wild dog
3. b. Swimming
4. b. 12 days
5. a. Fennec fox
6. c. Bat-eared fox
7. a. Central Asia
8. b. A pack
9. c. 90 cm
10. a. Ethiopia

Pages 74-75

Arctic fox
Simien jackal
Grey wolf
Fennec fox
Coyote

SOLUTIONS

Pages 78-79

Keyword: KOMONDOR

Keyword: BERGAMASCO

Pages 80-81

6	5	1	2	4	3
2	3	4	5	1	6
1	6	5	3	2	4
4	2	3	1	6	5
5	4	2	6	3	1
3	1	6	4	5	2

2	3	5	4	6	1
4	1	6	2	5	3
5	6	4	1	3	2
1	2	3	6	4	5
6	5	1	3	2	4
3	4	2	5	1	6

1	2	4	3	6	5
6	5	3	1	4	2
5	6	1	4	2	3
4	3	2	5	1	6
2	4	5	6	3	1
3	1	6	2	5	4

Pages 82-83

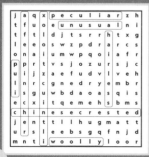

Pages 84-85

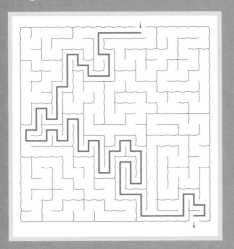

Pages 86-87

Page 88

1. a. Chow chow
2. c. Three
3. b. 1972
4. a. Sand skin
5. b. Ears
6. c. Hungary
7. a. Bedlington terrier
8. b. Neapolitan mastiff
9. b. Wire
10. c. Yodel

Pages 90-91

1 - 3 paw
2 - 6 tail
3 - 1 nose

4 - 2 tongue
5 - 4 teeth
6 - 5 eye

Pages 92-93

Shar pei
Chinese crested
Komondor
Chow chow
Bloodhound

Look for more puzzle books in this series!